Incredible Dumpling Recipes

Here's Your Way to Dumplings!

by Will C.

© 2022 Will C, All Rights Reserved.

Copyright Page

All rights reserved. No part of this publication can be distributed, reproduced, recorded, photocopied, or transmitted. If you desire to share or use this content for whatever purpose, you must seek prior permission from the author. Beware, the author will not be held responsible for your misinterpretation of this content or how your followers comment. However, it is fair to say that the content written herein is accurate.

Table of Contents

Introduction 5

What Ingredients Are Used in Making Dumplings? 7

   1. Steamed Dumplings Crispy-Bottomed 8

   2. Shrimp Dumplings 11

   3. Mantu` (Dumplings) the Afghan Beef 14

   4. Apple Dumplings Old-Fashioned 17

   5. Cornmeal & Chicken Dumplings 20

   6. Gnocchi & Chicken Dumplings Twin Made 23

   7. Curried Tomatoes Sauce with Chickpea Dumplings 25

   8. Herbed Dumplings with Vegetable Root Stew 28

   9. Chinese Dumplings aka Gyoza 31

   10. Jalapeno-Corn Dumplings with Pinto Bean Slow-Cooker Stew 34

   11. Creamy Peas and Bacon with Basil – Ricotta Cheese Dumplings 37

   12. Tamale Dumplings with Chicken-Chile Smoky Soup 40

   13. Corn-Dumpling Soup (Vori Vori) 43

   14. Tofu Dumplings 46

   15. Pierogis Potato 49

   16. Bacon and Dumplings with Chunky Fish Soup 52

17. Lime Custard with Golden Syrup Coconut Dumplings 55

18. Pink Peppercorns with Dumpling Noodle Soup 58

19. Hot Mustard Dipping Sauce with Deep-Fried Pork Dumplings....................... 60

20. Dumplings with Red Curry Sweet Potato Soup.. 62

21. Dumplings with Chili Oil 64

22. Prawn and Fish Dumplings with Noodle Soup.. 66

23. Dumplings with Italian Chicken Soup 69

24. Beans Soup with Paprika Dumplings... 71

25. Steamed Chinese-Style Dumplings 73

Conclusion 75

Biography.. 76

Thank you 77

Introduction

Dumplings are the perfect relaxation meal and a great way to explore the cookery world. Almost all cuisine features a form of dumplings in one way or another, and we love them—these all-feature dumplings from Chinese Dim Sum to Polish Pierogi and Caribbean Cornmeal.

Even if it is boiled, fried or steamed, doughy, savory, or sweet, clear is day eaten with a sauce or served in a soup, you will always find something you like about every or any type of dumpling. Our favorite collections of dumpling recipes worldwide have been put together here with its cooking guide.

Dumplings are now becoming extremely known across the globe. More people are trying more new and other exciting flavors, adding them together to create something entirely classy and unique dumplings that are completely tasty and textured.

Because of these experiments, however, the question would be, what are dumplings? It is not that simple to answer this question – but let us give it a try! In Asian Hostels and Restaurants, dumplings are bite-sized made of different wraps in a thin layer and delicate dough.

They are mostly sweet and savory and sometimes fried, boiled, and steamed – depending on how you want it. The Chinese know them as "Jiaozi" and "Gyoza" by the Japanese. Dumplings are a very popular Asian dish and are consumed with delight.

What Ingredients Are Used in Making Dumplings?

Dumpling dough comprises three key ingredients: water, salt, and flour. You have the option of choosing the flour you want to use; it depends on what type of dumpling you have in mind to make. But most standard dumplings are made of wheat flour. E.g., the Chinese shrimp dumpling, aka Har Gow, is made of mixed wheat with tapioca starch- and it's just the beginning. In the case of filling, dumplings are versatile, making them a great option, just like Bao Bun. Dumpling suits individuals with sweet teeth who would rather go for a savorer snack. Because you can prepare it anywhere you want it.

A Summary List of Dumplings Ingredient.

- Water
- Salt
- Flour (Any of your choice)

1. Steamed Dumplings Crispy-Bottomed

This recipe is of broccoli, butternut pumpkin sweet roasted.

Total Time: 1 – 2hrs

Servings: 4

Ingredients:

- 500g butternut pumpkin
- 6cm piece of ginger
- 1 tablespoon English mustard
- 1 lime
- 80g broccoli
- 1 tablespoon low-sodium soy sauce
- 1 teaspoon of red miso paste
- 2 spring onions
- 2 tablespoons sesame seeds
- ½ fresh red chili
- 1 tablespoon rice wine vinegar
- 24 x 10cmq sq. wonton wrappers
- 1 clove of garlic
- ¼ teaspoon of sea salt
- ¼ teaspoon of black pepper
- 2 tablespoons of oil

Instruction:

Preheat your oven up to 350°F, divide your pumpkin into 4pcs, remove the seeds, then toss with a single tablespoon of oil, add black pepper and a pinch of sea salt. Roast for 1hr on a tray until it becomes golden and soft. Then allow it to cool.

Get 2cm of ginger, peeled garlic, and broccoli, miso with vinegar, then blend until it's fine. Pour in the pumpkin, then season for taste.

One after the other, slowly wet wonton wrapper edges with your finger, include 1 heaped teaspoon filled with filling on the middle of each, and fold together to seal (don't worry if anyone tears in the process), put them in an oiled frying pan nonstick as you continue. Pour about 150ml water in the pan, place it on a stove, and cover. Allow it to steam until water evaporates completely. Open it and let it fry. Remove immediately the bottoms are and golden.

In the meantime, peel the remainder of the ginger, neatly grate it with chili and serve in a dipping bowl. Finely shred and trim the spring onions. Serve with lime wedges, soy sauce, and mustard. Then, sprinkle with sesame seeds toasted.

2. Shrimp Dumplings

Shrimp and cabbage dumplings are healthy, which makes an excellent huge batch. You can have some for lunch and dinner and refrigerate the remaining later. You can differentiate the dumpling filling, attempt ground turkey rather than the shrimp. Get wonton wraps in a cooling machine or fridge case. Serve with soy sauce.

Total Time: 1hr 20mins

Servings: 8

Ingredients:

- 1 ¾ pounds raw shrimp peeled & deveined (16-20 per pound)
- 1 ½ cups napa cabbage, chopped
- 4 teaspoons toasted sesame oil
- 1 ½ tablespoons finely chopped ginger
- 1 bunch chopped scallion
- 4 small cloves garlic, chopped
- 1 tablespoon reduced-sodium soy sauce
- ¼ teaspoon ground white pepper
- 8 teaspoons canola oil (divided)
- Cornstarch for sprinkling
- 48 wonton wrappers
- 2 cups warm water, divided

Instructions:

Add pepper, cabbage, soy sauce, scallions, shrimp, ginger, garlic, and sesame oil in a single food processor or grinding machine until well chopped.

Prepare the wonton wrappers, a little bowl with water, and a big baking sheet lined with baking paper sprinkled with cornstarch. On a clean working surface, fetch 1 tablespoon of filling into 6 wrappers in the center of each wrap. Use your wet fingers and rub them around the edges of each wrapper. Fold opposite corners towards the center of the so that they overlap, then fold the other opposite wrap in other to form a square. Then, you should press to seal in the center. Now place them on the baking sheet that has already been prepared.

To preserve an uncooked dumpling, place it on a baking sheet while on the parchment-lined until it becomes solid, for a minimum of 8hrs while it is open. Once frozen, move the dumplings into a freezer bag or airtight container, then put them back into the freezer.

When serving: Steam 2 teaspoons of canola oil in a huge nonstick skillet under medium heat. Put 12 dumplings (frozen or fresh) in a single layer, not touching and seam-side down. Pour ½ cup warm water into a pan. Cook while covered until the bottom side starts turning brown. Wait for about 60 seconds more. If needed, repeat the same process with water, dumplings, and oil.

3. Mantu` (Dumplings) the Afghan Beef

These types of dumplings are steamed and mostly served along with garlicky sauce yogurt, other chefs sometimes for flavorful, colorful counterpoint, tend to add tomato sauce to Mantu or dumplings.

Total Time: 50 minutes

Servings: 5

Ingredients:

- 2 teaspoons olive oil, extra-virgin-, divided
- ½ medium onion finely chopped
- 8 ounces beef, lean, ground
- 4 teaspoons grated garlic, divided
- 1 teaspoon grounded coriander
- ½ teaspoon grounded turmeric
- ¼ teaspoon grounded pepper
- ¼ teaspoon kosher salt, divided
- 20 pieces wonton wrapper
- ½ cup tomato sauce, without salt added
- ½ cup whole milk plain, Greek yogurt or labneh
- 1 tablespoon fresh mint nicely chopped
- 1 teaspoon dried mint

Instructions:

In a large skillet, heat a teaspoon of oil on medium heat. Put onion and boil, stir time to time, until it becomes soft for about 2 – 3 minutes. Put in beef with 2 teaspoons of garlic; continue cooking, make sure the meat is properly cooked, stir from time to time for about 5 minutes. Now pour into a bigger bowl and add coriander, pepper, 1/8 teaspoon salt, and turmeric.

On a clean chopping board, spread 4 wonton wrappers. Moist the edges of the wrappers with water. Place 1 little tablespoon filling in the center of each wrapper. Grab the corners of the opposite wrapper and hold them together for a few seconds. Do the same for the opposite, so all corners that meet at the center form a square pointed edge. Press the wrapper edges together for it to be sealed. Put the sealed dumplings on a baking sheet and close it with a damp towel. Redo the same process with the remaining fillings and wrappers.

Put a steamer basket into a large pot, add one inch of water, coat the basket with cooking spray. Place each dumpling in the basket, make sure it doesn't touch each other, and cover. Increase the cooking heat when boiling it for about 30 seconds, then reduce to medium heat and cook for 15 minutes.

Meantime, boil the remaining teaspoon of oil in a small pan under medium heat. Add a teaspoon of garlic and stir while cooking for 30 seconds. Add a pinch of salt and tomato sauce; simmer and cook for 5mins. After which, you can off the heat and cover to stay warm.

Combine yogurt or labneh with a pinch of salt and the reminder teaspoon of garlic in a small bowl. Spree the sauce on a serving plate and top it with tomato sauce. In order, place the dumplings on the sauce and top with dried and fresh mint.

4. Apple Dumplings Old-Fashioned

These apple dumplings are old-fashioned and a comforting dessert that reminds you of home. Just the way your grandmother would serve it, the dough is healthier, we have the whole wheat flour to thank for that, and the pastry is flaky and soft, just like the traditional dough. The apples melt in the mouth and are the perfect texture, and what completes this dessert is the cream yogurt mixture. Make sure you buy smaller apples; snacking apples, like the ones usually meant for kids, are great sizes for this type of recipe.

Total Time: 2hrs 5mins

Servings: 6, 1 dumpling, with whipped cream mixture 2 tablespoons each

Ingredients:

- 1 cup or 4 ounces whole wheat white flour, add a little more for work surface
- 5 tablespoons granulated sugar
- ¾ teaspoon kosher salt
- 3 tablespoons vegetable shortening, cubed
- 1 tablespoon canola oil
- 5-7 tablespoons ice-cold water, as required
- ¼ cup raisins
- 1 tablespoon honey
- 1 teaspoon grounded cinnamon
- 6 small or 4 ounces each peeled and cored tart apples (granny smith)
- 1 tablespoon water
- 1 large lightly beaten eggs
- 3 tablespoons heavy whipping cream
- 3 tablespoons low-fat vanilla-flavored Greek yogurt

Instructions:

Making the dough: Pour 2 tablespoons sugar, salt, and flour in a food processor until well mixed together, 6 -8 times. Include shortening; pulse until well mixed, and color resembles pea-size crumbles, 6 – 8 times. Add ice-cold water and oil, A tablespoon at a time, stir until a loose dough forms, 6 – 8 times. Transfer onto a dry work surface; Mold into a 5 by 7-inch flat rectangle. Wrap it with plastic wraps, then refrigerate for an hour.

Heat oven to about 350°F. Stir cinnamon, raisins, honey, and sugar all together in a small bowl and set it aside.

Open the wrapped dough and slice it into 6 equal pieces. Roll each piece of dough into a 5-to-6-inch square on the floured working surface. In the center of each dough square, place one apple. Each apple core should be filled with a raisin mixture. Pull dough up, one after the other and wrap the apple completely, pinch together dough at the top, brush tap water at the top to seal. Ensure to close all holes in the dough and press dough against the apple gently to help seal up.

Evenly brush dumplings with beaten egg. Place and arrange the dumplings in an ungreased 13 by 9-inch baking dish. In a preheated oven, bake until apples are tender, and pastry turns golden, which would take about 35 – 40 minutes.

Until a stiff peak is formed, vigorously whisk whipping cream by hand in a cold metal bowl for one minute. (On second thought, use an electric mixer to beat in high speed until it forms a stiff peak, for 30 – 40 seconds) fold in yogurt. Dumplings should be served with a dollop of the creamed whip at the top.

5. Cornmeal & Chicken Dumplings

This version of dumplings offers plenty of vegetables along with 5g of fiber per serving. It is made with 1 part of cornmeal and 1 part with flour, which makes these dumplings stand out from the usual dumplings. Which is healthier and a classic meal for a comforting dinner.

Total Time: 4hrs 15mins

Servings: 2 dumplings with 1 ½ cups of chicken mixture

Ingredients:

- 2 pcs medium carrots, thinly sliced
- 1 pc stalk celery, thinly sliced
- 1/3 cup frozen or fresh corn kernel
- ½ pcs medium onion, thinly sliced
- 2 pcs cloves garlic, minced
- ½ teaspoon chopped fresh rosemary or 1 teaspoon dried rosemary, crushed
- ¼ teaspoon grounded black pepper
- 2 pcs chicken thighs, skinned
- ½ cup fat-free milk
- 1 tablespoon all-purpose flour
- ¼ cup normal flour
- ¼ cup cornmeal
- ½ teaspoon baking powder
- A dash of salt
- 1 pc egg white
- 1 tablespoon canola oil
- 1 coarsely ground pepper

Instructions:

Add chicken, celery, rosemary, carrots, onion, garlic, ¼ teaspoon pepper, and corn in a 2 or 1 ½ quart slow cooker. In the mixture, pour the broth.

Close and boil on low for 7 – 8 hours or with high heat for 3 ½ to 4 hrs. In the case of heat, the setting isn't available. Boil for 5 – 5 ½ hrs.

When using low heat, increase to high and continue cooking. Now transfer chicken to a chopping board; let it cool off slightly. Slice the chicken meat off the bones; throw away the bones. Nicely chop chicken meat and return it into the mixture on the cooker. Combine flour in a small bowl and milk; mix properly until smooth. Pour into the mixture on the cooker and stir.

Make dumpling dough: Stir together ½ teaspoon of baking powder, ¼ cup of flour, a dash of salt, and ¼ cornmeal in a bowl. In a separate, Add 1 white egg, 1 tablespoon of canola oil, and fat-free milk in a small bowl. Transfer the egg mixture into the flour mixture and stir until it moistens.

Drop 2 spoons of dough in the 4 mounds into the top of your hot chicken mixture. Close and boil for 20 – 25 minutes or more until the inserted toothpick into the dumpling comes out neatly. (Don't lift cover while cooking.) Optional, sprinkle coarse pepper when serving.

6. Gnocchi & Chicken Dumplings Twin Made

In this recipe, we opt for tender gnocchi instead of homemade dumplings in this warming and richly vegetables and chicken stew recipe. The gnocchi remaining should be frozen in an airtight container.

Total Time: 35mins

Servings: 2

Ingredients:

- ½ cup thawed frozen peas
- 8 ounces shelf-stable gnocchi
- 2 ½ tablespoons flour, all-purpose
- 8 ounces chicken thighs, skinless, cut into 1-inch pieces
- 1/8 teaspoon salt
- 4 teaspoons olive oil, extra virgin, divided
- ¼ teaspoon pepper, divided
- ½ cup celery, sliced
- 1 cup carrots, diced
- 1 cup low-sodium chicken broth
- ½ tablespoon chopped fresh thyme (or a half teaspoon of dried thyme)
- 1 pc onion, diced

Instructions:

Boil water in a medium saucepan. Add and cook gnocchi, stir for 2 minutes. Now, add peas and boil until the gnocchi becomes soft, stir for 1 – 2 minutes more, then drain.

Meanwhile, toss flour on the chicken in a bowl until it's well coated. In medium-high heat, heat two teaspoons of oil in a skillet. Add the chicken into the pan, reserve the remaining flour in the bowl, and sprinkle 1/8 teaspoon of pepper and salt. Boil while stirring from time to time. Continue until it turns light brown, which should be between 4 – 5 minutes. Now move the chicken into a plate.

Now add the 2 teaspoons of oil into a pan. Add celery, carrots, thyme, onion, and the remaining 1/8 teaspoon of pepper; cook while stirring from time to time, until vegetables turn crisp-tender, which should be for 4 – 6 minutes. Now pour the reserved flour over the vegetables; stir to coat nicely. Now stir in the chicken and the broth. Boil, and stir from time to time until the stew becomes thick. That should be around 2 – 3 minutes. Add the peas and gnocchi and boil, gently stir until the gnocchi becomes hot. That takes about 2 minutes.

7. Curried Tomatoes Sauce with Chickpea Dumplings

This recipe was inspired by a dish served in India, Pakistan, and Afghanistan called "dharan ji Kadhi," The tender chickpea flour dumpling studs our rendition with greens and chiles. It's a healthy meal for a vegetarian because it has naan to sop up that sauce with a lot of protein.

Total Time: 45 minutes

Servings: 4 Dumplings with 3/4 Cup of Sauce

Ingredients:

- 1 cup + 2 tablespoons chickpea (garbanzo bean) flour
- 4 cups spinach or mustard greens, chopped and divided
- 1/3 cup and 2 tablespoons canola oil, divided
- ¼ cup nicely chopped red onion
- ¼ cup whole milk or plain yogurt
- ½ cup jalapeno or serrano pepper, nicely chopped
- ½ + 1/8 teaspoon salt, divided
- 1 teaspoon coriander seeds
- 1 teaspoon cumin seeds
- 1 tablespoon minced fresh ginger
- 1 teaspoon mustard seeds
- 1 tablespoon curry powder
- 1 can, 15 ounce tomato sauce, no salt added

Instructions:

Mix flour, 1/3 cup of oil, ½ cup of mustard green, ½ teaspoon of salt, onion, serrano or jalapeno, and yogurt in a large bowl. After which, make 16 dumplings using 1 tablespoon each into a nice shape.

Add the remaining 2 tablespoons of oil into a large skillet and boil over medium heat. Add cumin, mustard, and coriander seeds: close and cook until they begin to pop. That would be about 30 seconds. Stir in ginger and curry powder, add tomato sauce and tomatoes and its juice, stir nicely to combine thoroughly. Stir in the remainder 1/8 teaspoon of salt and 3 ½ cups of green. Let it simmer.

Nestle the dumplings nicely into the sauce, close, and cook, occasionally turning the dumplings and basting the sauce until it becomes soft, for about 20 minutes.

Tips:

Chickpea flour includes nuttiness and boosts the nutrition of these dumplings: Unlike the usual dumplings made with all-purpose flour, this boasts 2g more fiber in each serving. You can buy this flour in natural food stores or well-stocked supermarkets, or specialty flour is recommended.

8. Herbed Dumplings with Vegetable Root Stew

Herbed dumplings whole wheat dumplings served with vegetable root stew and nicely flecked with sausages. Make it the crowd favorite by adding sweet sausage or appetizing by using Italian hot sausage. The greens attached to a bunch of turnips and beets would be enough for this dish. Otherwise, use any leafy dark greens that look fresh and available at the market.

Total Time: 1 hour

Servings: 6 about 1 ½ Cups Stew and 3 Dumplings

Ingredients:

For Stew

- 4 teaspoons extra-virgin olive oil, divided
- 8 ounces Italian links sausages, sweet or hot
- 2 pounds assorted vegetable roots, peeled and diced (see tips)
- 1 large pc diced onion
- 4 pcs cloves garlic, minced
- 1 tablespoon fresh rosemary or sage, chopped
- 4 cups chicken broth, reduced-sodium
- 3 cups dark leafy greens, such as turnip or kale and beet, chopped

For Dumplings:

- 1 ¼ cups pastry whole wheat flour
- ½ cup cake flour
- 1 tablespoon fresh rosemary or sage
- 1 tablespoon baking powder
- 1 large lightly beaten egg
- ½ cup low-fat milk

Instructions:

Heat 2 teaspoons of oil over medium heat in a medium skillet to make the stew. Add sausages and cook until all sides turn brown, which should take about 5 – 6 minutes. Transfer to a clean chopping board. Let it cool a little, then chop into 1-inch pieces.

If parsnips are used, remove the woody part and quarter lengthwise before dicing. Heat the 2 teaspoons of oil left in an oven over medium heat. Add onion, stirring from time to time until it becomes barely tender, about 4 minutes. Add vegetable root and cook for 5mins. Add rosemary or sage and garlic and boil until fragrant for about 30 seconds. Add broth and let it simmer. Stir continuously.

To make dumplings: Meanwhile, whisk cake flour, sage or rosemary, baking powder, whole wheat flour, and salt in a bowl. Add milk and egg and stir to form a stiff batter.

After the stew reaches a simmer, stir in the sausage and dark leafy greens and return to a simmer. In the stew, drop the dough, 1 tablespoon at once, producing about 18 dumplings. Maintain heat for a gentle simmer by adjusting the heat, covering, and cooking uninterrupted until puffed. Sausage is well cooked, the vegetables are soft or tender, about 10 minutes.

Tip

Parsnips, carrots, and beets are peeled easily with a vegetable peeler, but for harder skinned roots like turnips, celeriac, and rutabaga, peeling with a knife is a lot easier. Create a flat surface by cutting off one end of the root and steadily keeping it on a chopping board. With your knife, follow the vegetable contour carefully.

9. Chinese Dumplings aka Gyoza

This dumpling recipe is originated in Japan and is fast and easy to prepare. It has a lot of folding methods. To make the Gyoza, Chinese filling are used.

Total Time: 40 mins

Servings: 5

Ingredients:

- 8 ounces grounded pork
- ½ cup Chinese chives or flat
- ½ small onion grated
- 3 tablespoons cornstarch + more for dusting
- 2 teaspoons Shaoxing rice wine
- 1 ½ teaspoons toasted sesame oil
- 1 ½ teaspoons soy sauce, reduced-sodium
- ¼ teaspoon salt
- 1 ½ teaspoons nicely chopped palm sugar or light brown sugar
- 1 cup chicken broth, low sodium, divided
- 2 tablespoons extra-virgin olive oil, divided
- 2/3 cup water
- 25 pcs Shanghai-style dumpling wrappers
- ¼ teaspoon grounded white pepper

Instructions:

Combine pepper, pork, sugar, chives, soy sauce, 1 tablespoon of cornstarch, sesame oil, onion, salt, and rice wine in a big bowl and mix well. Whisk the 2 tablespoons of cornstarch with water in a different small bowl.

Prepare your workspace with a small bowl of water and a stack of dumplings wrappers. With parchment paper, lay a large baking sheet and dust with cornstarch. Begin with 6 wrappers, add 2 teaspoons of filling in the middle of each. Run your wet fingers on the edges of the wrapper. Form a half-moon-shaped dumpling by folding the wrapper and pressing the edges together to seal. Crimp the edges if you wish. On the prepared baking sheets, arrange the dumplings without allowing them to touch each other. Repeat process with the remaining filling and wrappers.

Heat 1 tablespoon of olive oil in a large nonstick skillet over medium heat. In concentric rings, add half the dumplings, hugging each other and seam-side up, to get the pan filled. Boil until the bottoms are golden brown, for about 2 minutes. Add half of the whisked cornstarch mixture into the pan and pour ½ cup of broth. Cover and boil until the filling is well cooked and the liquid is nearly dried, that's about 5 minutes.

Using a spatula, make you use a nonstick pan to release the Gyoza easily. Using a plate slightly smaller than the pan, place the plate on the Gyoza upside down. Press with your 2 of your fingertips, then flip the Gyoza into the plate. (To avoid burning yourself, do not use the palm of your hands). Repeat process with the remaining olive oil, cornstarch mixture, broth, and Gyoza.

Tip

To prepare ahead: Uncooked dumplings should be refrigerated (step 1-2) for about 24 hours or frozen for about 30 days.

10. Jalapeno-Corn Dumplings with Pinto Bean Slow-Cooker Stew

This healthy bean stew recipe is enriched with veggies, bell pepper, onion corn, and celery and topped with chili crunchy bits of radish and cornbread dumplings and lime flecked. If you are out of time, kip the dumplings and serve the bean stew just as it is from the crockpot topped with a sprinkling of Monterey Jack cheese and tortilla chips crushed. Make sure your dried beans are soaked before boiling on the slow cooker to ensure it cooks well and on time alone with other ingredients.

Total Time: 5 hours

Servings: 8

Ingredients:

For stew:

- 6 cups water
- 1 pc medium onion, chopped
- 1 pound dry pinto beans, soaked
- 2 stalks celery, sliced
- 1 red bell pepper, medium, diced
- 2 cloves garlic, minced
- 1 cup corn, frozen and thawed
- 2 teaspoons ground cumin
- 2 tablespoons chili powder
- 1 ½ teaspoons salt
- 2 tablespoons lime juice

For dumplings:

- ½ cup all-purpose flour
- ½ teaspoon baking powder
- ½ cup buttermilk
- zest of 1 lime
- 1 pc fresh jalapeno, nicely chopped
- 2 tablespoons cold butter, slice into cubes
- ¼ teaspoon salt
- ¼ cup cornmeal, preferably whole-gain

Garnish:

- ½ cup freshly chopped cilantro
- ½ cup sliced radishes

Instructions:

Drain the soaked beans. Combine it with onion, cumin, garlic, celery, bell pepper, corn, chili powder, and water and cook over high heat for about 4 hours or 8 hours over low heat.

To make dumplings: Before your bean stew fully cooks, whisk cornmeal, baking powder, flour, and salt in a bowl. Use a fork or 2 knives to chop the butter and add it to the dry ingredients, then use a pastry blender to mix until it resembles a coarse meal. Add lime zest and jalapeno and toss to coat. Stir in buttermilk to form a dough.

When the stew is fully cooked, add salt and lime juice for 4 or 8 hours and stir. Using a large tablespoonful of dough, put 8 dumplings in the stew. Close and cook on high heat for 1 hour. Serve each plate of stew with dumplings at the top. Garnish with radish and cilantro.

11. Creamy Peas and Bacon with Basil – Ricotta Cheese Dumplings

This is a perfect dinner meal. Ricotta dumplings are mostly pan-fried until it turns brown and served with bacon or pancetta, creamy peas, and shaved parmesan. The Part-skim ricotta makes fluffy and light dumplings and adds protein to this classy and wonderful meal. See tip on making quenelles for a mess-free and easy way to shape the dumplings.

Total Time: 40 minutes

Servings: 4, 5 dumplings & ¼ cup sauce

Ingredients:

- 2 cups part-skim ricotta cheese
- 2 pcs large egg yolk
- ½ cup all-purpose flour + additional for dusting
- ½ cup fresh basil chopped and for garnishing
- ¼ teaspoon grounded pepper
- 1/8 teaspoon salt
- 2 tablespoons extra-virgin olive oil
- 1/3 cup chopped bacon or pancetta
- 2 pcs cloves garlic, chopped
- 1 cup frozen or fresh peas
- ½ cup light cream
- Pea shoots and shaved parmesan cheese for garnishing

Instructions:

Boil water in a large pot over low heat. Spread out a large baking sheet and dust with flour. Now with paper towels, line another baking sheet.

Stir ricotta, pepper, egg yolk, flour, salt, and basil together in a bowl until well mixed. Form 20 oblong dumplings out of the mixture or quenelles. Use 1 heaping tablespoon for each one. Assemble them on the floured pan.

Gently put the dumplings into the large pot of boiling water and cook until they float above the simmering water, about 2 to 3 minutes. Remove and transfer dumplings to the paper towel-lined pan with a slotting spoon.

Heat 1 tablespoon of oil over medium heat on a large nonstick skillet. Put In half of the dumplings and boil, stir once, until it turns brown for about 5 minutes. Move to a clean plate. Repeat process with the reminder dumplings and 1 tablespoon of oil.

Add garlic and pancetta or bacon to the skillet. Stir while cooking until fragrant, for about a minute. Add cream and peas. Cook and stir from time to time until thickened, for about 2 minutes. If needed, serve the dumplings with sauce, pea shoots. Garnish with parmesan and more basil.

Tips

Use spoons to mold your dumplings into quenelles or ovals. Fetch a dollop of the ricotta mix from one spoon to the other until you mold smooth football-shaped dumplings.

12. Tamale Dumplings with Chicken-Chile Smoky Soup

Tamale-like dumplings are pillowy and made with masa harina and toothsome bites of corny goodness and cheesy.

Total Time: 35 minutes

Servings: 6 with 1 ¾ cups

Ingredients:

For dumplings:

- 1 cup masa harina
- ½ cup low-sodium chicken broth
- ¼ cup shredded Monterey Jack cheese
- 2 tablespoons extra virgin olive oil
- ¼ teaspoon chili powder or ground cumin
- ¼ teaspoon salt

For soup:

- 1 tablespoon extra-virgin olive oil
- 1 cup chopped onion
- 1 ½ teaspoon chili powder or ground cumin
- 3 ½ cups chicken broth, low-sodium
- 2 cans or 15 ounces fire-roasted diced tomatoes
- 4 cups shredded cooked chicken
- 2 cups frozen corn
- 1 or 2 tablespoons adobo sauce mix with chopped chipotle pepper
- 1 cup sliced and quartered zucchini
- 2 tablespoons lime juice
- Lime wedges and chopped cilantro for garnish

Instructions:

To make dumplings: Mix masa harina, ¼ teaspoon of cumin or chili powder, salt, ½ cup of broth, 2 tablespoons of oil, and cheese in a medium bowl. Make 18 round dumplings by rolling the dough. Use 1 tablespoon of scant for each.

To make soup: Heat oil over medium heat in a large pot. Add cumin or chili powder and onion and cook for about 4 minutes until soft. Stir in broth, chicken, tomatoes with their juices, chipotle to taste, and corn. Let it boil over high heat.

Add zucchini and dumplings, reduce heat, close pot, and cook until the zucchini and dumplings are soft for about 5 -7 minutes. Now, add the lime juice. Serve the soup with lime wedges and cilantro on the side, optional.

13. Corn-Dumpling Soup (Vori Vori)

The word "Vori" means ball in the Paraguay language of Guarani; its plural form is Vori Vori. The name describes the ball shape of dumplings that floats in the broth. The soup is a fusion of the cuisines that originated from the Guarani people and the Spanish Franciscan missionaries. For the sleekest dumplings, use ghee, also known as clarified butter.

Servings: 6 cups

Total Time: 1hr 45mins

Ingredients:

For soup:

- 1 yellow onion, small and peeled
- 1 ¼ pounds bone-in chicken breast
- 1 pc small carrots
- 1 large pc clove garlic
- 1 pc stalk celery
- ¾ teaspoon salt
- 4 cups diced butternut squash
- 8 cups water

For dumplings:

- Scallion green or chopped fresh parsley for garnish
- ¼ cup white onions, grated
- 1 egg, large and an egg yolk
- 1 cup stone ground cornmeal
- 1 cup grated ricotta salata or grated queso Blanco
- 2 tablespoons unsalted butter or ghee, at room temperature

Instructions:

To make soup: In a big pot over high heat, put yellow onion, chicken, celery, carrot, garlic, and salt. Then add water. Let it boil with the cover on. Lower the heat to sustain a simmer. Cook until the thermometer inserted in the meat registers 165°F for 25-30 minutes. Cool the chicken while in the broth, about 8-10 minutes. Add the meat to a plate. Before returning broth, strain it and place it in a pot. (Dispose solids)

Meanwhile, whisk egg, onion, and yolk in a big basin with a fork. Add ghee, cornmeal (or butter), and mash to combine with a fork. Add knead and cheese till a dough forms. Close and allow it to rest—about 10 minutes.

Bring a big saucepan of water to boil in high heat. Shape 18 dumplings out of the dough, about 1 inch in diameter. Lower the heat to a simmer. Add half of the dumplings. Cook till they rise above the surface for about 5 minutes, then simmer for 4-5 minutes. Transfer them to a big plate. Repeat the same process with the dumplings still left.

Add a squash into the broth pot. Let it boil over increased heat. Reduce the heat to sustain a simmer, close, and cook till the squash becomes soft, 10 to 15 minutes.

Shred the chicken meat and return broth and dumplings.

Simmer for about 5 minutes. Serve with scallion greens or parsley at the top, if desired.

14. Tofu Dumplings

Tofu Dumplings are filled with nutrients, and the method of cooking this lovely dumpling ensures fewer nutrients are lost, which is by steaming. And it sure tastes good.

Total Time: 30 Minutes

Servings: 4

Ingredients:

- ¼ package (75g) soft tofu, sliced into cubes
- 300g minced vegetables
- ½ piece chopped green onion
- 150g minced pork
- 1 teaspoon salt
- 2 tablespoons vegetable oil
- 1 tablespoon minced ginger
- 1 tablespoon soy sauce
- 1 teaspoon chicken essence
- 2 tablespoons oyster sauce
- 2 tablespoons light soy sauce
- 10 pcs black fungus (Soak 4 hours in advance.)
- 300g flour
- 150ml water
- ½ teaspoon sugar
- 1 teaspoon sesame oil
- 50g vermicelli minced and cooked

Instructions:

In a wok, heat the oil. Add the oyster sauce, pork, light soy sauce, ginger, green onion in a big bowl, and hot oil.

Add black fungus, tofu, vegetable, sesame oil, chicken essence, salt, and sugar in the same bowl and stir well. Add pork mixture in other to prepare the filling.

Put flour in another bowl, gradually add water to the flour, and stir with a spoon. Move the dough on a lightly floured kneading surface and knead it nicely until it sets off smoothly. Allow the dough to relax for 30mins.

Make a 12-14 grams small dough. Then, press nicely to form a disc.

Fetch a tablespoon of filling and place it in the middle of the wrapper. Now use the wrapper to wrap the filling to form your dumplings.

Place your dumplings in the steamer and steam for 9-10 minutes. After that, put off the heat and cool down for 4-5 minutes. Now your dumplings are ready to be served.

15. Pierogis Potato

Pierogis Potatoes are the perfect comfort meal, and it is a cheesy mashed potato filling wrapped in a soft dumpling dough. And it doesn't take much time to make because it uses wonton wrappers instead of homemade dumpling dough.

Total Time: 45mins

Servings: 4

Calories: 291

Ingredients:

- 2 teaspoons extra virgin olive oil, divided
- ½ cup nicely chopped onion
- 1 cup cold mashed potatoes
- ½ cup or 2 ounces grated cheddar cheese
- Freshly ground pepper and salt for taste
- 24 to 28 pcs wonton wrapper, that's about 6 ounces
- 2 cups thinly sliced onions
- 2 cups sour cream, reduced-fat

Instructions:

On medium heat, heat 1 teaspoon of oil in a skillet; add the chopped onion and cook, while stirring until it becomes tender, for about 3 minutes. Move into a bowl and mix in cheese and mashed potatoes—season with pepper and salt.

On a chopping board lay a wonton wrapper. (Cover the remaining wrappers.) With a round cookie cutter, cut the wrapper into a 3-inch circle. Preferably serrated. Place 2 teaspoons of potato filling on one side of the middle of the circle. Rub the edges with water using a pastry brush. Wrap the wrapper over the filling and seal the edges together by pressing the edges. With tines of the fork, nicely flute the edges. Set the pierogi on a tray or baking sheets and continue adding pierogis until the filling is all used up.

Meanwhile, boil water in a large pot.

In a big nonstick skillet, heat the remaining 1 teaspoon of oil over low heat; add salt, sliced onions, and pepper for seasoning and cook, stir time to time until it caramelized and tender, for 10 – 20 minutes. (Add a little water or reduce the heat, to prevent scorching.) Adjust seasonings and taste. Put it aside and keep warm.

In boiling water, add salt and pour half of the pierogis. Cook until pierogis float above water and wrappers become tender. That should take about 3–4 minutes. Remove the pierogis using a slotted spoon and put them in the pan with onions. Do the same with the remaining pierogis.

Now place the pan containing onions and pierogis over low heat and shake the pan to coat the onions with the pierogis; warm through. Serve with sour cream immediately.

16. Bacon and Dumplings with Chunky Fish Soup

This incredible recipe will transport you on a culinary journey you haven't had before. You will surely enjoy yourself from the ingredients to the simplicity of instructions.

Total Time: 30mins-1hr

Servings: 6

Ingredients:

For soup:

- 2 tablespoons olive oil
- 1 medium onion, chopped
- 1 small red, capsicum (pepper), chopped
- 1 small zucchini, diced
- 150g (5 ½ ounces), chopped smoked bacon
- 1 clove garlic, crushed
- 2 tablespoons paprika
- 400g (14 ounces) chopped tomatoes
- 400g (14 ounces) chickpeas
- 450g (1 lb.) pike fillet, skinless, chopped into large pieces
- 2 tablespoons, chopped parsley flat-leaf (Italian)

For dumplings:

- 75g (2 ½ ounces) self-rising flour
- 1 pc egg, lightly beaten
- 1 ½ tablespoons milk
- 2 teaspoons nicely chopped marjoram

Instructions:

In a big saucepan, heat the oil, add onion. Cook over medium heat for 8 to 10 minutes, or till tender. Add the zucchini, garlic, capsicum, and bacon and boil over a reduced heat, often stirring for 5 minutes.

In the meantime, get the dumplings mixture ready by combining marjoram, milk, egg, and flour in a basin with a woody spoon.

Add the chickpeas, paprika, tomatoes, and water (800ml) to the legume in the saucepan. Let it boil over reduced heat and simmer calmly for 10 minutes, or till it condenses nicely. To form a dumpling, use 2 tablespoons to aid you. Add 6 oval shapes of the dumpling mix into the soup. Keep off for 2 minutes, then add the chopped fish into the liquid. Keep off for another 2-3 minutes, or better still, till the fish cooks thoroughly. The fish and dumplings should be simultaneously ready. Add spray parsley for taste, then serve.

17. Lime Custard with Golden Syrup Coconut Dumplings

These lime custards with golden syrup coconut dumplings are the perfect desserts. Have a look at our recipe below. You will come back asking for more.

Total time: 30mins-1hour

Servings: 5

Ingredients:

- 200g (7 ounces) plain flour
- 45g (1 ½ ounces) desiccated coconut
- 45g (1 ½ ounces) unsalted butter, chopped
- 55g (2 ounces) caster sugar (superfine)
- 125-170 ml coconut milk
- ¼ teaspoon salt
- Vanilla ice cream or whipped cream as needed

For lime custard:

- 500 ml or 2 cups custard
- ½ teaspoon nicely grated lime rind
- 1 tablespoon lime juice

Syrup:

- 40g (1 ½ ounces) unsalted butter
- 155g (5 ½ ounces) soft brown sugar
- 235g (8 ½ ounces) dark corn syrup or golden syrup

Instructions:

Pour the custard, lime rind, and lime juice into a medium bowl and combine well. Close with cling film and refrigerate till its required

Mix the coconut and flour in a big bowl, add salt. Then add butter and rub with your hands till the mixture looks like coarse breadcrumbs. Add sugar and stir. Use a bladed knife to create a hole in the middle. To make a tender dough, add enough coconut milk and mix well.

Add sugar, butter, 435ml of water, and golden syrup in a 9-inch large frying pan to prepare the syrup. Stir over reduced heat till the butter melts and sugar dissolves. Let it boil, then decrease the heat to simmer gently.

Add a teaspoonful of coconut mix into the heated syrup in a layer.

Close and cook over really low heat till the dumplings are properly cooked for 15 to 20 minutes. Allow to cool off a little. Then turn dumplings carefully over with a spoon into a serving dish. Serve with ice cream or whipped cream.

18. Pink Peppercorns with Dumpling Noodle Soup

This fresh and peppers riff on the wonton noodle soup goes perfectly well with beef dumplings.

Total time: 30 minutes

Servings: 4

Ingredients:

- 2 teaspoons pink peppercorns or (Sichuan peppercorn), freeze-dried
- 2 tablespoons chili sauce
- 250ml chicken stock
- 60ml light soy sauce
- ½ cup sake
- ¼ cup Chinese black vinegar
- 1 tablespoon brown sugar
- 1 tablespoon freshly grated ginger
- 20 pieces raw dumplings, store-bought
- 400g udon noodles
- ¼ teaspoon red bok choy (optional)
- ¼ teaspoon coriander, to serve (optional)

Instructions:

Put peppercorns in a saucepan over a reduced heat and boil, shaking the pan for about 2 minutes or fragrant. Add stock, soy sauce, sake, sugar, chili sauce, ginger, and black vinegar. Decrease heat and bring to simmer as you make the noodles and dumplings.

Prepare the noodles as instructed on the package and steam the dumplings. Separate bowls with about 3 to 4 dumplings per serve and scoop over the chili stock. Sprinkle red bok choy and coriander (if desired) and serve immediately.

19. Hot Mustard Dipping Sauce with Deep-Fried Pork Dumplings

These are perfect for a snack meal before the main meal. Not only do they look great, but they taste fantastic.

Total time: 30 mins

Servings: 4-6

Ingredients:

- 300g or 10 ½ ounces minced pork
- 4 pieces nicely sliced spring onions
- 1 tablespoon yellow mustard seeds
- 2 tablespoons light soy sauce
- 8 pieces water chestnuts, chopped
- 1 well-beaten egg
- 30 pcs gow gee (egg) dumplings wrappers, round or square
- 3 tablespoons English mustard
- 4 tablespoons oil, for deep frying

Instructions:

Combine spring onions, mustard seeds soy sauce, beaten egg, minced pork, and water chestnuts in a bowl. Mix well.

Place gow gee on a flat and dried surface and brush the edges with wet hands. Pour 2 teaspoons of the pork mixture into the center of the wrapper. Fold over to close the fillings in a semicircular or triangular shape. Firmly pinch together the edges to seal. Repeat the process with the remaining ingredients.

Prep sauce: Pour English mustard into a bowl, add 4 tablespoons water, then gently stir until it becomes smooth.

In a wok, heat oil and deep fry your dumplings in batches for about 1 to 2 minutes, or till golden brown and filling is cooked properly. Drain and serve it hot with dipping sauce.

20. Dumplings with Red Curry Sweet Potato Soup

This recipe brings out the best of both worlds, sweet and savory. With the burst of ingredients and recipes, you are bound to love these incredible dumplings.

Total time: 30 minutes

Servings: 6

Ingredients:

- 12 to 16 (450g) quality store supplied raw dumplings

Soup:

- 400ml coconut milk
- 700g sweet potato, chopped into 1-inch pieces and peeled
- 3 tablespoons red curry paste
- 400ml chicken or vegetable stock

To serve:

- ¼ red cabbage, shredded
- 1 bunch broccolini, halved
- ¼ cup coriander leaves, chopped
- 1 spring onion, nicely sliced

Instructions:

Pour curry paste into a big saucepan and cook (medium-high) till fragrant and oil starts separating. Add sweet potato. Boil for 1 minute before including the stock.

Let it boil over high heat. Then decrease the heat and let it simmer for 25 minutes until it softens. Put off the heat, pour coconut milk. Blitz with a blender till smooth.

Simmer the dumplings and broccolini as instructed on the packaging.

Serve the soup and top with 3-4 dumplings in each serving bowl. Add the raw cabbage, broccolini, coriander, and green onion. Serve immediately.

21. Dumplings with Chili Oil

The title of this is exciting enough. Having some dumplings with chili oil sounds like the perfect idea for a cold winter night. Indulge!

Total time: 30 minutes

Servings: 6

Ingredients:

- 16pcs square wonton wrappers

For the filling:

- 250g minced pork
- 1 tablespoon grated ginger
- 1 small, beaten egg
- 1 tablespoon oyster sauce
- ½ teaspoon sesame oil
- A pinch of salt and pepper

For the sauce:

- 1 tablespoon chili oil
- 1 teaspoon sesame oil
- 1 tablespoon soy sauce
- 1 teaspoon caster sugar

Instructions:

Add minced pork, sesame oil, grated ginger, egg, oyster sauce, and a pinch of salt and pepper in a big bowl. Mix properly using your hands till it becomes smooth.

Spread the wonton wrapper on a neat baking paper. Fetch 1 teaspoon of filling in the middle of the wonton wrapper, one after the other. Rub the edges and fold over with a wet finger to make a triangle. Seal the edges by pressing gently. Repeat process till all 16 dumplings is over.

Cook the wonton in a big pot of boiling water for about 2 minutes till they float over the water. Then drain. Mix the sesame oil, chili oil, sugar, and soy sauce. Serve immediately.

22. Prawn and Fish Dumplings with Noodle Soup

If you love prawn fish, then these prawn and noodle soup dumplings will blow your mind. Have a look at the recipe below!

Total time: 30 mins to 1 hour

Servings: 4

Ingredients:

- 5 liters (52fl ounces or 6 cups) chicken stock
- 100g (3 ½ ounces) vermicelli noodles
- 1 teaspoon fish sauce
- 2 tablespoons soy sauce
- 2cm (3/4 inch) fresh ginger, bruised and peeled
- 1 tablespoon Chinese rice wine (optional)

Prawn and fish dumplings

- 100g (3 ½ ounces) raw king prawns, peeled, cleaned, and chopped
- 200g (7 ounces) white fish fillets, skin, boneless, and chopped
- 50g (1 ¾ ounces) sugar snap peas, nicely sliced
- 1 pc white egg, lightly beaten
- 1 tablespoon Chinese rice wine (optional)
- ¼ teaspoon white pepper, ground
- Sea salt, as needed

Extra ingredients for adults:

- 2 tablespoons soy sauce
- 2 long red chili, nicely sliced
- 1 bunch bok choy (500g or 1 lb. 2 ounces), chopped
- 2 pcs spring onion, nicely sliced

Instructions:

Line parchment paper on a baking tray.

Prepare prawn and fish dumplings: Place the prawns and fish in a processor and mix to form a paste. Then, transfer into a big bowl, add rice wine, egg white, and sugar snap peas. Season with sea salt and white pepper. Combine them well. Fetch a teaspoonful of the mixture into your hands, roll it into balls, and place it nicely on the baking tray. Continue the same process until the mixture is finished, then refrigerate to firm slightly for 15 minutes.

In the meantime, in a heatproof basin, pour the noodles and hot water and allow it for 2 minutes, or till noodles soften. Drain water and keep aside.

In a large saucepan or pot, pour fish sauce, stock, rice wine, soy sauce and ginger, then let it boil through high heat, decrease the heat to a simmer. Now add the dumplings. Simmer for about 6 minutes. Bring out the ginger and add the vermicelli noodles and stir.

Serve with extra ingredients as desired.

23. Dumplings with Italian Chicken Soup

This soup will revolutionize your taste buds. It's made with Italian chicken, which is always delicious.

Total Time: 45 minutes

Servings: 4

Ingredients:

- 350g (12 ounces) minced chicken
- 75g (2 ¾ ounces) or 1 cup fresh breadcrumbs, fully packed
- 70g (2 ½ ounces, 2/3 cup) nicely grated parmesan cheese
- 1 ½ tablespoons chopped & rinsed capers
- 2 tablespoons basil
- 1 egg yolk
- 25 liters (44 ounces) chicken stock or chicken consommé good quality
- 2 tablespoons parsley (Italian) flat-leaf, to serve
- ¼ teaspoon salt
- ¼ teaspoon black pepper (ground)

Instruction:

To prep the dumplings: with your hands, mix entire ingredients except for parsley and egg yolk in an average size bowl and mix well. Season with black pepper and salt. Now add the egg yolk and mix well.

Fetch a teaspoonful of the mixture, then roll into balls with your hands, placing the dumplings on a tray or plate nicely in a single layer while you roll. Close and refrigerate till required.

Bring the stock to simmer gently, add dumplings and cook over reduced heat until properly cooked or 10 minutes. Serve instantly, with the parsley on top.

24. Beans Soup with Paprika Dumplings

The bean soup and paprika dumplings will take your dinner to the next level. They are made with precision and the perfect ingredients. You will absolutely love this recipe.

Total Time: 30mins

Servings: 4

Ingredients:

- 1 tablespoon light olive oil
- 1 medium onion, chopped
- 3 cloves nicely chopped garlic
- 1 tablespoon Hungarian paprika
- 1 pc medium potato, chopped
- 1 pc medium carrot, chopped
- 200g flat beans, sliced into 2cm length
- 400g borlotti beans, cooked
- 1 liter vegetable stock
- 1 pc egg, lightly whisked
- 1 tablespoon chickpea flour (besan)
- 2 tablespoons plain flour
- 2 teaspoons Hungarian paprika, extra
- 2 tablespoons lemon juice

Instructions:

Heat the oil in a big saucepan, add garlic and onion over reduced heat until the onion turns golden.

Add the paprika and stir for a minute. Add the flat beans, carrot, and potato and boil for 5 minutes.

Add the stock and borlotti and stir. Cover and simmer over reduced heat until tender or 5 minutes.

Whisk the egg, the extra paprika, and flours in a medium bowl, and stir together. Put 1 teaspoon at a time of the mixture into the soup and bring to a simmer. About 2 minutes or till the dumplings are properly cooked. Off the heat, add lemon juice, and stir. Dish out with garlic bread.

25. Steamed Chinese-Style Dumplings

This recipe of dumplings is common as a cool starter at my place. They are nicely served as part of a bigger Asian dish, leaving other diners impressed at the effort.

Total time: 1-2 hours

Servings: 3

Ingredients:

- 2 pieces chicken breast fillets, or 4 pieces thigh fillets
- 1 bunch coriander, including stalks, chopped
- ¼ cup water chestnuts drained, sliced, roughly chopped.
- 3 pieces green shallots, white, and a little green part, nicely sliced
- 1 small knot fresh ginger, nicely chopped
- 2 teaspoons sesame oil
- 1 tablespoon soy sauce and extra for dipping sauce
- ½ tablespoon rice wine (optional)
- 2 to 3 small pieces red chilies, halved lengthwise, thinly sliced
- 1 packet (150g) egg wonton wrapper
- 2 tablespoons extra-light oil, for greasing

Instructions:

Chop chicken nicely to create a rough mince. Pour in a large bowl, then use your hands to mix chestnuts, coriander, green shallots, soy sauce, ginger, sesame oil, rice wine, and half of the chili. If you are using chicken breast, add light oil (1 tablespoon). Now use a tablespoon to fetch the mixture and roll it into balls using your hands. Place each ball in the middle of the wonton wrapper, topped with slices of chili, and bring the wrapper sides around the filling to form a shape of a money bag. Repeat process entire mixture, wrappers, and chili.

To cook, have a skillet ready with 5cm of water to simmer, or enough to be just below a when put into the skillet. Dip the lower part of the dumpling into the light oil and put in the steamer in the skillet and close to cook. Ensure the lid covers the skillet properly so that steam doesn't escape. Steam dumplings in groups of 8, or as many as your skillet can contain without sticking together for about 6 minutes.

Make about 20 dumplings with this ingredient and serve with soy lime dipping sauce.

Conclusion

Well, there you have it, our very long dumplings recipe cookbook. We hope you will have fun with all of our recipes made very easy with locally available ingredients. Take time with your family to prepare the dumplings as it's super fun and a great way to bond with each other.

Enjoy!

Biography

Food is like music, and Will knew that when he stepped into the restaurant business. Will loved food, and American classics were always a favorite. He loved the feelings and emotions some of this food invoked in him. Serving unique American dishes was one way to connect his love for music and food on a plate. Customers who would later come into his restaurant could instantly link classic American music stars to the food on their plates. This was a thought well appreciated by the diners.

Even more was that Will researched old and deep-rooted foods in American history, added his spin, and gave the customer a piece of history on the plate.

However, his career did not start in the food industry, but after working as a waiter in a couple of local and renowned All-American restaurants, he went back to culinary school to perfect his skills in plating dishes to aesthetically please the customers as they listened to music from back in the days.

Customers came to his restaurant not because he was a good cook, but to learn the American story behind the meals.

Today, Will has ventured into other food terrains, including serving original cocktails that pair incredibly well with steak and others. He has a restaurant and is making a difference in the lives of his customers.

Thank you

Did you like my book? I pondered it severely before releasing this book. Although the response has been overwhelming, it is always pleasing to see, read or hear a new comment. Thank you for reading this. And I would love to hear your honest opinion about it. Furthermore, many people are searching for a unique book, and your feedback will help me gather the right books for my reading audience.

Thanks!

Will C.

Printed in Poland
by Amazon Fulfillment
Poland Sp. z o.o., Wrocław
11 April 2022

9c01f4a3-f563-4058-80e5-145869fe7118R01